Whatever your situation, I feel confident that you will find something in here that will have the power of unleashing positive changes in your work and home life.

www.fast-print.net/store.php

FROM STRESS TO SUCCESS
Copyright © Hansa Pankhania 2014

All rights reserved

No part of this book may be reproduced in any form by photocopying or any electronic or mechanical means, including information storage or retrieval systems, without permission in writing from both the copyright owner and the publisher of the book.

The right of Hansa Pankhania to be identified as the author of this work has been asserted by her in accordance with the Copyright, Designs and Patents Act 1988 and any subsequent amendments thereto.

A catalogue record for this book is available from the British Library

ISBN 978-178456-044-7
e-Pub ISBN 978-178456-826-9
Mobi ISBN 978-178456-827-6

First published 2014 by
FASTPRINT PUBLISHING
Peterborough, England.

Contents

5 Short Stories from the Workplace

Built for Resilience - We all have the ability to be resilient and perform at our peak; each and every one of us, including you. Read how Paul overcomes adversities and does this despite working in a high pressure environment.

To Change or not to Change - Change is normal, nothing remains constant in life. This is a story of Mike who resisted a major change with serious consequences and Lisa who embraced it and turned it to her advantage.

Rushes of Anger - Never let anger build up until it turns to destructive behaviour and compromises your relationships and career. That's what happened to Joe Barnes, but be got back on track. Find out how he does it in this story.

The New Man - The inspiring tale of the transformation of Neil, a senior executive on the verge of a nervous breakdown.

The Mediator - We all experience conflict at work with colleagues or bosses. This should not mean that we leave the job, or bear and put up with it. There is a way out and Paula and Mo find out what that is in this tale.

Each story is accompanied by a handy commentary packed full of expert guidance and tips.

All the tips and techniques are passed on in good faith and the author and associates are not responsible for any contraindications.

Welcome

Every so often there is a story highlighted by the media about stress issues affecting a famous person - actress has breakdown, international sportsman diagnosed with depression etc. The silver lining to these worrying stories is that it raises awareness of the severity of these problems and, as a result, perceptions are changing for the better.

Of course, it's not just the rich and famous who experience stress-related issues. Stress is the number one cause of workplace absence in the UK. In 2012, stress accounted for three times as many absences as back pain (International Stress Management Association).

There is a raft of self-help books out there that can give you guidance on how to overcome stress and perform at your peak. So why should you read this one as opposed to all the others?

This collection of workplace short stories is written from experience and inspired by our clients. These stories are based on real life scenarios and interventions, in a way that protects and respects our client confidentiality. As such, it doesn't always mean that at the conclusion of the tale everything is rosy in the garden and everyone lives happily ever after. Real-life isn't like that. However, these stories will resonate with many of you and give you tips and techniques to help you overcome common, as well as complex, problems. It will also make for an interesting and exciting read.

Real life situations and real life interventions, written with our first-hand knowledge. Hopefully you will be helped to see that the small investment in these interventions saves long term costs and enhances profits. I feel confident that you will find something in here that will have the power of unleashing positive changes in your work and home life.

Enjoy.

About the Author

Hansa Pankhania is a Corporate Wellbeing Consultant and Trainer, as well as a Senior Counsellor and Executive Coach. She is a Fellow of the International Stress Management Association and one of their eight validated trainers/consultants in the UK.

Her passion for Stress Management and Wellbeing began when she researched stress for her thesis at University and began to develop training programmes on this and related topics. Although her formal training is in western psychological and organisational models, she uses a unique approach combining eastern wisdom and concepts into her programmes.

She worked as a consultant and trainer for top consultancies in the UK and in 2005 set up and became director of AUM Consultancy. At Aum

Consultancy, she and her team of twenty associates are passionate about making a positive difference to individuals and organisations. They are dedicated to enabling people, employees and organisations to overcome stress-related challenges and reach their peak potential using simple and practical approaches.

In this book Hansa draws on her extensive experience of working with individuals and private, public and voluntary sectors. The stories are inspired from her day-to-day work and contain powerful messages and coping strategies on five different areas: stress management, resilience building, anger management counselling, mediation and change management.

Please visit www.aumconsultancy.co.uk or call us on +44(0) 121 6049821/ +44(0) 7888 747438 and find out how we can support you too.

BUILT FOR RESILIENCE

Paul walked back to his desk. It was Friday afternoon, and in just over an hour he'd be driving home, looking forward to a few drinks and a Saturday morning round of golf. His 30th birthday was just under a month away and he was excited about planning a big night out with his golf friends to celebrate. Paul also had this niggling unsettled feeling in the pit of his stomach. His moments of calm and happiness were few and far between, but at least he had a couple of things to look forward to this weekend. He sat at his desk and checked his emails. Friday afternoon was usually a very quiet time for his Inbox, so he was surprised to see that he'd received two new emails in the five minutes since he had last checked. He considered ignoring them until Monday; after all, what could he possibly do at 3:30pm on a Friday that couldn't wait until 8:30am on Monday? His curiosity got the better of him and he reluctantly opened the first of his new messages:

"I've decided I don't want to talk to you at the minute. You just end up making me upset. It's both of our faults, but quite frankly I'm better off without you at present. Please don't call me this weekend. Besides, I'm sure you'll be too busy getting drunk and hitting a ball around a field to give a toss about me anyway!

Take Care, Kate x"

Kate had been Paul's girlfriend for five years, they had a house together and for a long time, seemed the perfect couple. But over the last year, the relationship had been strained. Privately, Paul knew that it was largely his fault. He'd been fed up with his job at Crest; he had been promoted from the sales team and was a 'Sales Team Manager'. He had much preferred the cut and thrust of being a salesman; Sitting behind a desk all day carrying out admin tasks wasn't really Paul's thing. Give him a customer and a product and he was well away, but give him ten members of staff and he wasn't very good at motivating them or organising their working days.

It wasn't what he expected; Paul had fancied the idea of being a people manager, a chance to inspire, to pass on his sales knowledge, plus he'd be earning a few more quid! Unfortunately, the role wasn't what he had been hoping for. The recession was slowing down sales, he missed the art of selling and he found the paperwork mind numbing. His manager had spoken to him on various occasions about his performance, and at his previous monthly appraisal he had been told that his performance was under review. This meant that if it carried on he would be in line for a formal warning and possibly worse.

As a result, he had been experiencing long spells of unhappiness and had been argumentative. Kate had borne the brunt of Paul's bad moods, and their relationship had deteriorated. Three weeks ago she decided she'd had enough, packed her bags and moved back in with her mum. Paul hadn't made much of an effort to stop her, they needed some time apart. Besides, he'd actually enjoyed the time he'd had to himself. He'd missed Kate, but her absence had meant more nights out with friends, more sport on the TV and more rounds of golf. He didn't want to split up with Kate, but he was happy with the current arrangement for a little while longer.

Paul debated whether or not to reply to the message. In the end he resisted the temptation to say something sarcastic and decided to respect her wishes and not communicate with her. Besides, it would just make him angry. Message two was very odd:

"Paul,

Top news! We've got a bit of budget to spend and I thought it'd be great to send you for some coaching. Don't worry it's not finding out about some boring spreadsheets or learning a new program. As we've discussed in your one-to-ones, you've been finding things tough over the last few months, but I have every faith in your ability.

So, I've decided that you could benefit from some Resilience Building training. It's in-house and aimed at helping you to perform at your peak despite our high pressure culture, to feel better about yourself and ultimately be a better manager. I can vouch for the effectiveness of the sessions, and I think you'll find them highly beneficial. You should have an email from the company with full details of content, times etc., I expect the first session will be in about two weeks.

And don't worry about missing time at your desk, Jen will look after things. We'll brief her next week. I'll also send you a meeting invite soon, so we can discuss this and what I want you to get out of it.

Actually I wish I was going myself!

Mal"

Paul slumped back in his chair. He considered his options for getting out of the sessions. Illness? Too obvious, besides he'd had a week off 'sick' recently. True, he hadn't technically been unwell, but he'd been feeling overwhelmed by the job and decided a few days at home were in order. Holiday? Non-starter, he only had a couple of days left to book for the year, and he needed them for Christmas. He wracked his brains for some more ideas, but couldn't think of a plausible option. It looked like he was going to have to go.

Paul spent most of his final hour of work in a bad mood. He was still in a funk as he drove out of the car park. He'd never really understood the point of this type of coaching - whatever you chose to call it - aimed at improving your wellbeing or building resilience. Surely it was just a case of getting a grip and riding out the bad times. He didn't need some new age person telling him what to do. How was that going to improve the sales figures? He found some heavy rock music on his iPod and played it at a high volume for the duration of his drive home.

By the time he got home, Paul had decided on the most suitable course of action for the evening – get drunk and try to forget about his upcoming misery. He had planned to meet his best friend Adam at their local pub that evening, but that was two hours away. That seemed like an eternity, so he decided to get started early and have a couple of cans of strong ale before going out. He put a ready meal in the microwave, got changed out of his suit and settled down for a couple of hours in front of the TV. Paul thought, "A few beers, a lasagne and Deal or No Deal are all I need to feel relaxed!"

"All I'm saying is that there's no harm being open minded about it." Adam put his pint glass on the table and looked at Paul. They had been friends for over fifteen years and Paul felt comfortable talking to Adam about anything going on in his life. Since Kate had moved out, he'd found Adam a great help in keeping his spirits up and offloading his problems. Adam was one of those people who seemed to find life easy. He was married, ran his own business and seemed to be going off on holiday at least once every few months. Nonetheless, he was a great friend and Paul was comfortable talking to him about anything.

"OK, I'll admit that things have been a bit stressful lately. I mean, I've lost my girlfriend and I hate my job. Who wouldn't feel stressed out?"

"Yeah, but this is a great chance to sort it out. I just think it's worth a try."

Paul looked unimpressed. "I'm just going through a rough patch. A few beers is all the therapy I need!"

Adam laughed. "If only that were true. A few pints and all your problems go away."

"That's how it works."

Adam raised an eyebrow. "For a few hours maybe. But wake up tomorrow and you've still got your problems." He pointed at his half empty pint glass. "This isn't the solution."

"Hmm, that seems a tad hypocritical."

"Not at all. I drink 'cos I enjoy it and it's sociable. It's not 'cos I want to solve anything or forget about stuff."

Paul looked at his friend thoughtfully. "Well that's lovely, but I've got a load of stuff I want to forget about and this is a great way of doing it. Same again?"

Paul pointed to his glass and got up to go to the bar. As he waited to be served he thought about Adam's words. He had been drinking a lot lately, largely because he wanted to forget about work, Kate and the moribund state of his life. Still, he was sure it was just a phase and he'd be back on track soon enough. 'Wish You Were Here' came on the jukebox. It was one of his favourite songs, but it wasn't really what he wanted to hear at that moment.

When he returned to Adam, they chatted about football, music and a film they had both recently watched. For a short while, Paul forgot about his problems and all was well with the world.

The office of Mal Lovell was rarely visited by the employees of Crest. Mal was a well-respected manager and preferred to adopt the 'less is more' approach to running the show. If you were summoned to his office, you knew it had to be something important. So it was with some trepidation that Paul knocked on the door. It was the day before his Resilience Building training started and Paul was expecting a thorough grilling on what he was expecting to get out of the sessions. Mal didn't disappoint him.

"Ah Paul, all set for tomorrow?" Mal was sat behind his desk, arms folded and with a stern look on his face.

"I think so. Just need do a quick handoff."

Mal raised an eyebrow. "That wasn't exactly what I meant Paul. I was talking about your prep for the training."

"Oh, they haven't sent me any prep work to do."

"And you didn't think to use your initiative, find out more about it and work out what you wanted to get out of it?"

Paul paused. He was bang to rights, but didn't like to admit it. "Well, I was going to have a read up tonight and have a think on the drive in tomorrow".

Another raised eyebrow. "Is that so?" Mal unfolded his arms and leant forward. "Look Paul, I don't spend money on training like this for nothing. It costs a lot of money and it means we've got a Sales Manager out of office during busy periods. These sessions are vital to your future with Crest. We need you performing at your best, and that means we need you happy, calm and motivated."

Paul felt a bead of sweat forming on his forehead. He'd barely given the training a second thought over the last few days. The only positive he could see from it was that it was time out of the office. Since he'd received the 'invite', he'd had far more pressing issues to deal with. Kate hadn't been back in touch, his team's sales figures were reaching new lows and he had been feeling increasingly despondent. He was finding it hard to sleep. He was having angry outbursts at work, at home and when he was with friends. The last thing he needed now was to listen to some hippy mumbo jumbo.

"I'm sorry Mal. I've had a lot on lately."

Mal sighed. "That's part of the problem. You're letting it all build up. I can tell just by looking at you. You're not sleeping, you smell of booze and your team are looking unmotivated and bored. You're meant to be inspiring them. Not making them want to leave."

Paul felt like a naughty schoolboy. Mal hadn't raised his voice, but Paul could tell he wasn't happy. Nonetheless, he couldn't really see what he could do in the next few days to turn things around.

"OK, I'm sorry. I'll give this my full attention. I'll work hard and I'll get my team's figures up."

"That's what I want to hear. Now make sure you do what you say you're going to do."

As Paul set off the next morning, he had a heavy sense of foreboding, he hated training and this one had a very high chance of not only being boring, but also making him feel extremely uncomfortable.

He parked up and made his way to the meeting room that had been designated for the first session.

By the end of the first session, Paul had slightly revised his opinion of Mal's decision to put him forward for the training. It wasn't life changing, but he had to admit Jane the trainer knew what she was doing and knew how to engage the audience. During the first session he got to like Jane, she really believed in what she was passing on and spoke with passion and humour.

"Resilience is about the ability to bounce back from adversity in the shortest possible time. When you are resilient, you are calm, relaxed, focused, happy, in control, highly effective, making good decisions, energetic, healthy, approachable and cheerful. It is possible to be this way most of the times in our lives, regardless of the challenges, we may be facing. Every one of us, including you, has the ability within to be resilient, and we can all learn to do so using simple, and practical methods. My aim is to ensure you fully understand the concept of resilience and make simple and practical changes that will increase your resilience considerably."

To Paul's surprise, he was finding himself nodding along to Jane's eloquent delivery. Nonetheless, he still retained a degree of scepticism about how this was going to improve his life. That scepticism remained until lunchtime, when he decided to take himself off to the park across the road and spend some time on his own. He sat on a bench gazing out at the green space bathed in sunshine, and mentally checked out his resilience levels. His thought train was interrupted by a female voice.

"Mind if I join you?"

It was Jane. She was carrying a cup of herbal tea and looked totally relaxed.

"Go for it," Paul replied. "It's a lovely spot."

Jane sat down and for about a minute they sat in silence gazing out at the gorgeous scenery. Eventually, Paul decided the silence was getting awkward.

"I enjoyed this morning. Lots of good stuff."

Jane smiled. "Thank you. I've been doing this job for about eight years and I still love hearing positive feedback."

"Yeah, it's been far more interesting than I expected."

Jane laughed. "Well, listening to me talking isn't going to solve all your problems. If I could do that, I'd be rich, famous and sitting on a beach in Hawaii.

Sadly, life's more complicated than that. Often, the biggest step is realising that you can make things better."

"Can I? My girlfriend's left me, I hate my job, I drink too much and I feel unhappy most of the time."

"You probably think I'm making this up to make you feel better, but a friend of mine was in a similar place a few years ago. She worked for a multinational company who didn't give a stuff about her, she split up with her husband and was smoking about forty fags a day."

"And then she had an epiphany and suddenly everything was great?" Paul realised he sounded sarcastic, but this was exactly the type of tale that made him cynical about this type of training.

"No." Jane looked offended. "That doesn't happen. As it goes, she had to work bloody hard to get back on track. She had to take risks and make sacrifices. But you know what? She now does a job she loves, has just got engaged, stopped smoking and has even started writing music."

Paul was impressed by the passion in Jane's voice. Maybe there was a way out of his rut. However, it was her final words that piqued his interest. He had also wanted to be involved in music and loved listening to people talk about their experiences of song writing and performing.

"Writing music? What sort? Does she play live?"

Jane grinned. "I knew I could make you listen eventually! She used to play in a band, they were fairly big. Folky type stuff. She was the guitarist. Did a few festivals and released a couple of singles. But they split up when they all started getting married and having kids. Now she's in a good place and thought she'd give it another bash. I listened to some of her stuff last week. It's early days and she's just getting a few ideas down and coming up with tunes, but it sounds really good."

"Brilliant. I'm a mere sales manager. Always wanted to work in music but my mother was dead against it. Consider me jealous."

"I don't want you to be jealous. I want you to be inspired." With that, Jane got up, announced that her tea had gone cold and walked off, leaving Paul feeling a combination of inspired, slightly embarrassed, but oddly happy .

His next session with Jane was a couple of days later, this time he found himself 'in the zone'. A phrase he liked to use when he was completely focused on something. He'd heard athletes refer to being 'in the zone' during races and felt that it applied just as well to his life. Paul felt at ease talking about his problems and frustrations. It felt like a great weight being lifted off his shoulders.

If the initial session was about self-realisation for Paul, then the subsequent ones were about beginning to find solutions and ways forward. Jane's guidance had made him realize that it wasn't going to be easy, but with some effort he might just be able to get there.

"To be fully resilient we need to pay attention to all parts of ourselves, physical body, mind, emotions, relationships and life purpose in equal measure. If you are not doing this then can you still expect to continue to function at your peak at all times?"

"Hmm" said Paul, "I must have been neglecting most parts of me from what you say."

Later on, Jane explained how to achieve optimum resilience by following the five steps that involved nourishing our physical body, mind and thoughts, emotions, relationships, and life purpose.

"Let's now talk about nourishing your physical body."

"That sounds like you want me to eat loads. I can tick that box already."

Jane laughed out loud. "Not exactly, I'm talking about stopping your bad habits. Instead of having a few beers when you get home from work, why don't you try going for a long walk?"

"I don't really enjoy long walks."

"Well no, but it's just an example. You could read a self-help book, eat healthily, go for yoga or Pilates, meditate or go to the gym. I'm just saying that there are better ways to nourish your physical body than a few cans of lager. Try a few and you might find yourself thinking more clearly and positively."

When it came to the end of the training, Paul personally sought out Jane to thank her for the sessions and wish her the best for the future.

That Friday night, he met Adam for a couple of drinks.

"So how did it all go?"

"I really hate saying this, but you were right."

"You mean you enjoyed it?"

"Yeah, but not just that. It's really opened my eyes to where I'm at and what I need to do. Got some cracking tips and ideas. I'm actually excited about the future."

Adam made a grand gesture of feeling around under the table and looking at Paul's ears. "Are you wearing a wire?"

"Huh?"

"Well, there are two options here. Either you're an imposter and the real Paul Mason has been kidnapped, or this is some kind of wind up and Jeremy Beadle is about to walk in."

Paul grinned. "For a start, Jeremy Beadle died a few years ago so that seems unlikely. Secondly, I don't have any rich friends so there wouldn't be much of a ransom if I was kidnapped. Thirdly, I'm being honest. It was great. Really inspired me and made me think."

"Seriously mate, I'm chuffed for you. So what's made you suddenly feel so positive?"

"Like I said, got loads of tips and ideas. For example, don't laugh, but I've started meditating every day."

Adam did laugh. "Now that I would love to see!"

"It's great. I just spend ten minutes in the morning with my eyes closed focusing on calm images and words. Really makes me feel relaxed and ready for the day. Also whenever something is bothering me, I write it out and don't bottle it up. Works wonders!"

"That's great Paul. So what's the plan?"

"Well, the reason I'm a sales manager in an office is because I applied for the job and I was the best person for it, so there's no point getting down about that. After all, I wouldn't have got the role if the bosses didn't think I was up to it. What I need to do is turn the situation to my advantage, do the best job I can and show my boss what I'm made of."

"Brilliant to hear that mate. And Kate?"

"I've been an idiot. I've been unfair to her and I don't deserve her...But if there's a chance to get her back and make up for everything then that's what I'll try and do." Paul delivered the words with a steely determination, for the first time in ages he was feeling positive and knew actually what he wanted.

Six months later, Paul once again found himself being summoned to Mal's office. However this time he didn't feel intimidated by the prospect of facing his manager. This time he felt calm and confident.

"Paul, come on in. How's it going?"

"It's going well." Paul wasn't lying. His sales results for the last quarter had improved considerably, his team had been performing much better and he was up to speed with all of his paperwork and admin.

Mal broke into a rare smile. "That's what I like to hear. A happy worker is a good worker. I've always had faith in you. I'm glad that you've now got faith in you." He looked at the paperwork on his desk. "To be honest Paul, it's all positive from me. You are meeting all your targets, your staff are happy and you seem to always be in a good mood. I'm really pleased for you mate. How's the home life?"

"Fantastic, Kate's moved back in and we've just booked a holiday to Portugal for Christmas."

"Good to hear it, look mate, we need to have a chat soon about a role that's come up at head office. There's a bit of competition out there, but I think you'd have a chance."

"That's great, I love a challenge. Can you send me the details?"

"Will do. And Paul...keep it up."

Paul walked out and headed back to his desk. He had one new email. To his surprise it was from Jane.

"Paul,

Hope everything is well and you're in a good place. Got a bit of a proposition for you. Do you remember my friend who was trying to get back into the music business? Well it's really taking off and she's played a few gigs. Anyway, she's getting some great feedback and has decided to record some tracks and release them.

The thing is...she needs a manager. It's not a full time job, but it'd be some weekend and evening work. Meetings with producers, bookings, PR, marketing etc. I know you're into that kind of stuff. Let me know if you're interested and I'll pass on your details.

Jane"

Paul's eyes lit up. There really was something to this Resilience Building malarkey.

Commentary

Paul's story is typical of many people in today's fast-paced society. He experienced a difficult change of role at work. Unfortunately he didn't have sufficient coping mechanisms to manage the situation. He let everything get on top of him, and subsequently his performance at work and happiness at home were adversely affected. There is a difference between the buzz people get from doing a busy and challenging job and an unreasonable pressure which can harm personal wellbeing. In Paul's case, his circumstances led to unhappiness and arguments. In other cases it can lead to exhaustion and burnout. This happens when we keep overusing our body, not taking time out to nourish all aspects of it, and feeding it with the wrong products.

Paul's situation highlights the importance of being resilient as challenges and adversity are part of life, we all have to face them. But how do we continue to bounce back and perform at our peak levels despite that? Paul's course helped him to do just that by paying attention to all aspects of his being (the human machine).

Imagine a machine, what would happen if you did not maintain all of its parts and fed it the wrong product? It will begin to work less effectively and eventually break down! This is what was happening to Paul.

These are the 5 steps that Paul was helped to follow on his journey to resilience:

Step 1 - He started off by attending to his physical body. He cut down harmful products such as excessive alcohol and replaced these with nurturing routines like walking and meditation.

Step 2 - He then addressed his thoughts and the health of his mind by learning the art of positive thinking and the law of attraction which is about attracting positive outcomes through positive thinking and visualisation.

Highly resilient people have a realistic, optimistic view of the world. They tend to operate from hope of success rather than fear of failure. We all have setbacks in life but it is believing that we can overcome these that creates positive outcomes.

Think of a challenge that you have faced. What was your belief about it? Did you believe that you will overcome it? Was it positive or negative?

For example, if Paul believed that he would never make it as a Sales Manager and will eventually lose his job, what might have been the consequence of this belief? Jane and Mal helped him to believe that he can be good in his role, which is one of the factors that helped to turn things around for him.

The following will help you to develop a more positive attitude:

A) *Become more aware of your negative self-talk (e.g. I am no good at this, I am a failure etc.)*

B) *Get into the habit of thinking with a positive 'can do' attitude*

C) *Always set positive goals.*

Psychology research has found that focussing on a positive goal is much more effective than focussing on a negative goal as **positive thinking leads to** *positive emotions, positive action and positive outcomes.*

Step 3 - Paul learned to deal with his emotions by writing them out using the therapeutic writing template as below.

I feel frustrated because......

I feel sad because.....

I feel angry because.....

I feel hurt because......

I feel positive because.....

I feel happy because........

Step 4 - He recognised the importance of healthy, fulfilling and supportive relationships and made a commitment to build these with his girlfriend Kate and spend time with his friends who were willing to help.

Do you have a network where you have regular practical, psychological and moral support?

We look at how to develop this in our Anger Management story.

Step 5 - What would happen if you had a natural flair and talent in something that was not nurtured and developed and you were forced to do the opposite? A good example is someone who has a flair and passion for art but has to train and work as an accountant in their family business. Would this person perform at his/her best?

Is your work fulfilling?

What do you need to do to be aligned to your true life purpose in order to make life more meaningful?

Paul did this by taking up the opportunity to pursue his music. Live your passion and help others to do the same as Jane did for Paul.

R NOT TO CHANGE?

Change is often used in popular culture. There are numerous well known phrases that include the word and plenty of famous songs referring to change. It's usually seen as being a positive event – 'A change will do you good', 'a change is as good as a rest'. Even Paul Weller seemed happy about the fact he was a Changing Man.

Mike Collins reflected on this as he sat in his living room gazing absently at whatever soap opera his mother happened to be watching. His opinion of change certainly wasn't positive. Three months ago, he'd been a team manager at Grafton Market Research Agency. He was in charge of a team of ten people, whose job was to ring up the public and ask those vital questions such as what newspaper they read, who they would vote for in a General Election and how many hours of TV they watched every week. Mike thought it was a pretty good job. He enjoyed preparing reports for Grafton's head office, as well as supervising his staff. They were a combination of students and long term workers – and the team were successful. That was until Jill turned up from Head Office one day.

There were two teams in the office, performing similar roles. As well as Mike, there was another team manager – Lisa - who looked after a similar team. Mike and Lisa got on well and had a strong working relationship. In fact, they had just been for a lunchtime drink to discuss staff turnover, when they walked into the office to be greeted by Jill.

"Come through," she said, pointing to a nearby meeting room. "There's something we need to discuss."

Jill then explained that, due to budget cuts and new management, they were relocating the offices thirty-five miles away. This meant they'd be letting the short term members of staff leave. In addition, the new office would only have fifteen market researchers. This meant that both Mike and Lisa's roles would be altered. Previously, they were asking experienced team members to carry out tasks such as compliance checks and complaint handling. Now, they would have to do it all themselves. Even worse, they were being asked to fill in on the phones during busy periods.

Since that fateful meeting, Mike had grown disillusioned with Grafton. They were messing his life around. He'd worked hard to get where he was and he didn't want the upheaval. He was also worried that he wouldn't be able to cope with the new role. He'd never worked in telephony before, he always tried to avoid it. What if he wasn't as good as the people he was managing? Plus, there was the additional travel and the fact that the new office was in the middle of nowhere. It all added up to a situation Mike was dreading.

He'd assumed that his mother would be understanding and help him through the change. However, her view was that Mike should just get on with it. Arguments became the norm and they both withdrew from each other. Hence, why Mike now found himself sat in front of the telly pondering the merits of change, worrying about his job and dreading the fact that it was just two days to go until the move happened. Earlier mornings, menial jobs and a load of disinterested workers.

"I need a smoke," he muttered, before trotting off to the kitchen and rolling himself a joint.

"That's right." His mother shouted after him. "Have a spliff, that'll solve everything. If you have enough then all your problems will just go away."

Mike used to enjoy his mother's sarcastic comments, now they just annoyed him. He took a drag. It was disgusting and he screwed up his face, took a deep breath and exhaled. He wasn't entirely sure when he'd made the change from drinking for pleasure to taking drugs out of necessity. It had probably coincided with his insomnia. He squeezed his fist tightly and slammed it on the table. "It's this sodding move. Life was great until that point." He took another drag. In the absence of any other solutions, this would have to do.

As expected, the move went terribly for Mike. He hadn't fully realised how much longer his drive to work would be. He had to get up an hour earlier every day. "Doesn't matter, you don't sleep much anyway." His mother said, completely missing the point.

The extra travel wasn't the main problem though. Mike found his new tasks unbearable. He was spending large chunks of his time conducting surveys, something he loathed and found utterly demeaning. On top of that, his new team consisted of young, intelligent, post-graduates looking for some easy money before getting a 'proper job.' None of them were going to be there for longer than a year, but they all thought they had better ideas on how to run things. Mike was being bombarded with ideas on how to make the office more efficient. He wasn't interested; he just wanted to get through the day, go home, have a smoke and forget about how miserable his job was.

The nadir came when Brad, one of the graduates, sent him an email suggesting a new way of putting together the staff rota. There had been a few moans from staff, that the current system was unfair. Complaints ranged from 'I've got to work late on Friday, two weeks in a row,' or 'I need to start later on Wednesday 'cos I need to take my Nan shopping.' As it turned out, Brad's suggestion for making it fair was a very clever and fair one. However, Mike was in no mood to accept that some scruffy student was more intelligent than him, so he just declined the idea and told Brad that it wouldn't work.

At that week's team meeting, it became clear that Brad's suggestion had made its way around the entire office. Mike was subjected to a flurry of questions about the new system and, more specifically, why he was opposed to it. Mike found himself spouting off a number of increasingly absurd excuses for not changing the rota. Eventually, after Mike had made a childish comment about there being a spelling mistake in Brad's email, a couple of members of staff simply got up and walked out of the meeting.

"Where are you going?" Mike asked.

The reply came from Chloe, a usually shy and reserved girl. "I'm sorry, but I've got a job to do. This is just silly. We're wasting time and not getting anywhere." With that she calmly walked out of the room, taking two other workers with her.

All eyes turned to Mike, he felt suitably embarrassed, but also defeated. There was no fight or desire left in him. "Err, let's just call it a day shall we. We can pick up next time. Back to work everyone."

After four months of this misery, Jill arrived at the office for a meeting with Mike. Mike had been dreading this moment, he was fully aware that he'd been late submitting reports, his call stats were poor and he'd had a couple of recent absences. He was fully expecting a dressing down, but not quite to the extent that Jill gave him.

"It's unacceptable, we need to address this situation." She said calmly, but with a stern look on her face. "I've suggested that you needed to have some help, but you haven't responded." I've had three separate emails in the last week from members of your team complaining that you've been rude to them. Also, that you've been leaving early and not managing the team fairly."

Mike squirmed in his seat.

"Sorry, it won't happen again, just a few teething problems."

"I understand that there would be some teething problems. One complaint from a member of staff could be unfortunate, but three?!" Her voice was raising and Mike started to feel the sweat forming on his forehead.

Jill continued, "As you haven't been interested in taking my advice, I've decided to move over here for a few weeks. We'll need to work together in addressing your issues. I'm going to oversee things, take a bit of the pressure off you, but also to monitor your performance. There needs to be changes. I know you didn't like us moving offices, but there's nothing we can do about that."

Mike slumped back in his seat. So this is what it feels like to hit rock bottom.

"Come through," Jill said, pointing to a nearby meeting room. "There's something we need to discuss."

Lisa Grant and her colleague Mike followed Jill to the meeting room, where Jill proceeded to tell them that their jobs would be changing pretty dramatically. As she digested the news, the prospect of change had filled her with dread. What if she couldn't cope with the role? What if she ended up managing a load of disinterested students looking to do as little as possible? And she certainly wasn't looking forward to the extra travelling.

Lisa was relatively new to her role. She had been promoted from the telephony staff six months previously. She loved managing a team and trying to meet targets. She had ambitions of going higher in the company and even running her own business one day. This news was putting a huge question mark over her plan. It was going to be far harder to move up the corporate ladder now that her responsibilities were going to dwindle.

On her way home, she stopped off at her local library to return a couple of books that were approaching their due date. Lisa had always been open minded about life, so decided to have a little look to see if she could find any books that might be able to help with her current situation. After a few minutes, her eyes fell on one entitled "How to Cope with Change". The author had a name that Lisa couldn't even begin to try and pronounce, but the title really grabbed her. She decided to give it a try and see what she could learn.

For the next few evenings she worked her way through the book, making notes and discussing some of the themes with her boyfriend. After finishing the book, she felt altogether more confident about the upcoming change and had some ideas that she wanted to put into practice.

To try and calm her nerves, she went for lots of long walks and discussed the matter in-depth with her boyfriend. They agreed to make changes to their daily routine. He would get the bus to work so she could have the car and save some time. In return she would pick their son up from school twice a week when she could leave work early.

As suggested in the book, Lisa put her concerns into two lists. Things she had control over and ones she did not. Lisa then arranged to have a couple of meetings with Jill, to discuss her concerns and areas where she could gain more control. Jill was impressed by Lisa's honesty. The one to one meetings helped her to identify her training needs for the new role. She made a plan to prepare and learn the skills needed. She also decided to keep an open mind and ask for help in the areas she found challenging. Finally, she made a point of making a couple of visits to the new office prior to the move. Not only did this help her get a good idea of how long the journey took, it also allowed her to familiarise herself with the new surroundings. The new premises were actually more spacious, had excellent new equipment, air conditioning and there was a lovely Garden Centre and Cafe at the end of the road. She was confident that she could cope with the change in location, but it was the change in role that was going to be more challenging.

Initially following the relocation, Lisa was stressed. She wasn't adapting easily to the new work schedule and her new team. She would take short breaks to practice some of the relaxation techniques she had picked up from the book. It was a great help and she found she had the mental strength to persevere and settle into the new role.

The extra travel was a bit of a shock to her system and was proving to be tiring. By the end of the week, she would be overwhelmed, so she would meet up with friends and talk through her problems. She also joined a yoga class to ease her stress.

After four months or so, Lisa realised she had settled into the new role and was feeling a lot happier about her job. Her performance had not only returned to its pre move levels, but she was actually exceeding Jill's expectations.

At the end of the quarter, Jill made a visit to the office and asked to see her in the meeting room. Lisa was usually a bit nervous when Jill visited, yet on this occasion she felt confident. She had far exceeded her targets for the month, her staff were performing well and she had even grown to enjoy conducting her own surveys. With that in mind, she was a bit concerned by Jill's opening words.

"I'm afraid things haven't quite gone to plan since we've moved offices Lisa."

"Oh, how do you mean?" Lisa was confused.

"We're going to have to have a bit of a rejig. Unfortunately, Mike has been struggling since the move, so I'm going to be moving over here for a few weeks, mainly to give Mike some guidance but also to assess how the office is performing."

Lisa felt anxious, she knew that Mike had been underperforming, but the way Jill was talking seemed to indicate that she wasn't happy with the way the whole office was working. Jill noticed Lisa's nervous look.

"Don't worry. I'm absolutely delighted with how you are getting on. In fact I want you to take on some of Mike's work, particularly the management side of things. Do more appraisals, run meetings, look at new ideas and so on. It's a great chance for you to learn new skills. I can see you stepping up a level in the future."

"Wow." Lisa was taken aback. In truth, she was a bit uncomfortable with receiving praise, but this was music to her ears.

"And there's more." Jill reached down into her bag and pulled out a colourful folder. "We've had four separate emails into Head Office from members of your team praising you." She passed the folder to Lisa. "I've printed off the emails. Oh, and there's a little something extra in there as well."

To Lisa's amazement she had won the company's Top Performer award, which meant being rewarded with a sizeable bonus and meant that instead of spending her two weeks annual leave pottering around the Cotswolds, she could look forward to sunning herself in the Algarve. Now that was a change she was certainly looking forward to.

Commentary

This story highlights how Mike and Lisa approached and reacted differently to change. Mike reacted negatively and failed to adapt to his new work pattern. Lisa, whilst at first apprehensive, tackled the situation positively which resulted in a great outcome.

For a few moments imagine what the world would be like if nothing ever changed. Hopefully you will see that change is a normal part of life as most things do not remain constant. Change is inevitable, therefore it is how you deal with it that is vital to your happiness and success.

Think of a change that you have faced in life, what was your approach to it?

Was it one of the following?

- ***Resistance*** *- refuse to accept it, try and change it back to how it was before.*

- ***Survival*** *- accept it to a point and put up with it.*

- ***Growth*** *- accept it, adapt to it, and enable positive outcomes.*

Lisa's approach was the third one, she grew from the opportunity that the change provided. She did this by applying the 4 C's from her Change Management Book. These are:

- **Commitment** - This is about 'committing' to the change and dealing with it step by step. Mike was fearful, saw the change as a threat, and shied away from it. He did not face the change, he avoided it and remained in denial.
- **Challenge** - Approach every change as an opportunity for growth not as a danger or bad omen. Change is an opportunity to learn new life skills and grow stronger as a person. Lisa learned many new skills that led to a promotion and increase in confidence.
- **Control** - Change has aspects that we can control and others we have no control over.

Think of a current or forthcoming change and make two lists of all the issues and tasks of what you have control of and others that you do not. Now, work with each issue in the 'cannot control' list and explore possible solutions with the help of your support network.

Lisa did just that with her boyfriend, friends, Jill and staff team.

- **Communication** - For Mike, the communication broke down with his mother at home and with his team. On the other hand Jill handled the change well by communicating with her staff on a regular basis and offered support as required. Lisa also talked to people at work and home and did not hesitate to ask for help.

Of course, it's not always as simple as just applying the 4 C's to a situation. Major and constant multiple changes can be overwhelming. It is vital therefore to draw on our resilience skills as well to maximise our personal resources and coping ability.

Here is a quick summary of the 5 Steps to positive change outcomes

- *STEP 1 - Face the change, do not avoid or deny it.*

- *STEP 2 - Approach it as an opportunity for growth.*
- *STEP 3 - Nourish your physical body, think positive, let go of negative feelings. (Refer to Commentary on Built for Resilience)*
- *STEP 4 - Separate what you can control, focus on this and let go of what you cannot.*
- *STEP 5 - Communicate with others and seek information and support as needed.*

Now apply the 5 Steps to the change that you are undergoing and look forward to enhancing your strength and repertoire of skills.

RUSHES OF ANGER

Joe Barnes had a highly unusual problem. He was stood in the bathroom at the house of his local member of parliament, with a copious amount of blood running from the back of his left hand. Joe took a deep breath and tried to think what to do.

Two hours earlier, he had been sat at his desk at the Sotherton Gazette, trying to write an article on the proposed by-pass for the town. The proposal had been met with complaints by local residents who were concerned that it would create noise pollution and ruin local businesses. His feature for the following day's edition was about the pros and cons of building the new road. So far it largely comprised of quotes from local shop owners and a couple of interviews with members of the council. It was hardly looking like an award winning article. Joe welcomed the interruption when the phone rang giving good news, his request to interview the cabinet minister responsible for the by-pass proposal had been swiftly met. A short drive later and Joe found himself sat in the drawing room of Vanessa Granger MBE and Member of Parliament for Sotherton. Joe's day and article were looking a lot brighter, but it was then that his troubles began.

Vanessa Granger had been friendly enough and happy to answer some preliminary questions about her recent work and even made a few comments about her personal life. However, when the conversation moved on to the proposed by-pass, she started to become uncooperative and abrupt.

"I'm not prepared to comment on that at this moment," was her standard response to any question about the road. She wouldn't give any opinions on the proposal or even comment on how the proposal was developing. Joe was becoming increasingly frustrated and annoyed. He decided to try one last gambit.

"So, can you give us any indication of when a final decision will be made on the road? It's something our readers, and indeed all local residents, are desperate to know."

"It's too soon to say. I'm sorry; I can't give you an answer on that."

Joe slumped back in his seat, his heart was thumping and he could feel his face turning a bright shade of red. "Err, excuse me, I just need to pop to your bathroom for a moment."

Joe felt the rush of anger in his body, his steps faltering and making him feel faint as he made his way to the bathroom. Once inside, he slammed the door shut and punched the wall as hard as he could. He immediately regretted his action. He was hit by an intense pain and wanted to scream at the top of his voice. The more pertinent problem was the blood that was appearing on his hand. He had no idea how he was going to explain that to Mrs Granger.

In truth, it wasn't the first time that Joe's anger had spilled over in recent weeks. Three days earlier he'd smashed a plate on his kitchen floor after a bad day at work. Just that morning he had almost crashed his car on the way to work after getting annoyed with a slow driver ahead of him. This was an altogether more serious situation though. He frantically tore off reams of toilet paper and wrapped it tightly around his hand in a desperate bid to stop the blood. It helped to an extent, but there was still a trickle coming out from his knuckles. He washed his hands in the sink and dried it with even more toilet roll. "This will have to do," he thought, "she's going to wonder what I'm doing in here."

He nervously made his way back to Vanessa Granger and proceeded to ask a couple of inane questions about some issues in the town. Not surprisingly, she had started staring at his hand. Joe decided to try and explain the situation.

"Oh, it's a sports injury that's flared up. I play cricket at the weekend, last week and got hit on the hand whilst batting."

He immediately realised his mistake.

"Weren't you wearing gloves?"

"Umm....no, it was during practice and I was just messing around, hitting a few balls. Silly really, should always wear gloves when a cricket ball is heading your way."

She didn't look convinced, but must have decided it wasn't worth pursuing the matter. The interview ended shortly after and Joe said his goodbyes and made his way out to his car.

"What am I going to tell the boss?" Before leaving for the meeting he had triumphantly told his editor that he was off to get an exclusive interview with Vanessa Granger and get her views on the by-pass proposal. He sat in his car and looked over his notes. The main nuggets from the interview were that she was in favour of gay marriage, liked playing badminton twice a week and enjoyed listening to Pink Floyd. It wasn't exactly screaming

'Exclusive' at him. All of a sudden his frustration boiled over and he thumped the steering wheel and screamed. A few seconds later he was aware of Vanessa standing by the next car looking out at him. "Great, she's going to think I'm insane," thought Joe. He pretended not to notice her and did his best to drive off calmly.

The most important time of the week for the Gazette was 1:00pm on a Friday. All of the writers gathered in the boardroom and Chief Editor Jerry Pickford finalised the content for that week's edition. Being a weekly publication, there were only six full-time employees and they each had to cover a variety of topics. In addition to being a features writer, Joe also had to write restaurant reviews and the television section of the paper. It was the features that he regarded as being the most important part of his job. He had always wanted to be a journalist and his ambition extended far beyond the confines of Sotherton. He was approaching his fortieth birthday and was desperate for a national newspaper to give him an opportunity, but he realised that time was running out. In truth, this had been the source of his recent anger outbursts. He had done his time with the Gazette and needed to move on. He didn't want to spend his Friday lunchtimes listening to Jerry explaining that there would be a four page feature on a farm show in that week's paper.

"We were going to lead with the Lottery winner story," explained Jerry. "But our very own Joseph Barnes has just returned from a meeting with Vanessa Granger so we may have a last minute change to the front page."

Everybody looked at Joe.

"Err yeah, it was an interesting discussion."

"Did you get all the lowdown on the by-pass?"

Joe explained that no, he didn't get the lowdown on the by-pass. In fact he didn't get much of a lowdown on anything.

"She likes badminton and Pink Floyd?" Jerry asked. "How on Earth is that going to be front page news?"

"We could use 'cock' in the headline. That seems apt." It was Ray Broad, the sport's writer for the paper and constant source of annoyance for Joe. Ray never missed that chance for a sarcastic comment and seemed to particularly relish winding up Joe. He had been the one to pen the story of the local resident who had recently won

£3,000,000 on the National Lottery. The story that was currently going to be front page of the next edition.

"Thanks for that Ray. Any more clever remarks?"

"Comfortably dumb?" Ray suggested this with a smirk on his lips, getting a bigger laugh from the rest of the room.

"Oh, just shut up Ray," snapped Joe. "I've had illnesses more amusing than you. You're thirty, you live with your parents and look like a hippy student with anorexia. If anybody should be getting laughed at here it's you." The anger was boiling up inside him, but before it could go any further Jerry slapped his hand on the boardroom table.

"Joe, I think you better go outside for a bit and calm yourself down. Ray, less of the wisecracks. We're here for serious work not to listen to your stand-up comedy routines."

Joe stormed out of the room and straight to the smoking area behind the building. He didn't smoke, but often came out here to just try and calm himself down. "Christ, I need a new job," he thought. "I'm fine away from here, this place is driving me insane"

Jerry poked his head out of the door. "Joe, we need to have a chat. What happened in there isn't acceptable. I know Ray can be a pain, but there's no reason to react like that. We're far too busy to deal with it this afternoon, so make sure you finish off the piece on Granger, then go home. I want to see you first thing on Monday." With that, Jerry went back inside, leaving Joe to contemplate his future.

"C'mon Joe. Let's get an early wicket mate."

It was Saturday afternoon and Joe was doing what he enjoyed the most; playing cricket for Sotherton. In his former years he had been a talented fast bowler and had almost made it as a professional. Twenty years later, his hair was receding and he ached for days after playing, but he could still bowl effectively for his local team and was preparing to open the bowling in the first league fixture of the season. His first ball was exactly what he hoped it would be, the batsman made a nervous attempt to play the ball, missed it and the ball thudded into the wicketkeeper's gloves.

"Great start Joey. Keep it there," shouted one of the fielders. Joe looked at the batsman, a young man, fresh out of university and aiming to make a name for himself. In return he received a smile and a stare. Joe read this as a sign that this guy wasn't afraid of him and felt he could score runs off him easily enough. "We'll see about that," he thought.

The next ball, Joe decided he would try some intimidation. He delivered a bouncer aimed at his head. He steamed in to bowl and hurled the ball down the pitch as fast as he could. The batsman calmly ducked under the ball and stared back at Joe, the same slight smirk on his lips. Suddenly Joe was imagining the batsman was Ray Broad, rival journalist and all round annoyance, not just some cocky, young upstart. "Revenge" thought Joe. Revenge for the way Ray had spoken to him the previous day.

For the rest of the over, Joe tried his hardest to bowl as fast as he could and hit the batsman somewhere on his body. Unfortunately, the batsman was more than up to the challenge and comfortably dealt with the attack, even despatching one ball to the boundary for four.

At the end of the over, Joe's captain trotted over to him. "Great pace, but try and pitch it up, he likes the bouncers. Try and do what you did with the first ball."

Joe was barely listening, this had become personal. 'Ray' needed to be taken down a peg or two and a cricket ball was just the thing to do it with. Two unsuccessful overs later, his captain had had enough. "What are you doing Joe? He's taking you to the cleaners; you're just bowling a load of rubbish. Sorry mate, I'm taking you off. We can't keep conceding these runs."

Joe was seething, you could almost hear the sound of his teeth grinding, he hated failure and he hated being told he wasn't performing.

"Give us one more over. I can get him out."

"Sorry Joe, you need a break."

Somewhere deep within him, Joe felt he may be right, but found it difficult to admit that.

"Need a break? You don't know what you're doing! I'm your best player by a mile."

"Joe! You're not bowling anymore, I'm in charge here and that's my decision."

"Well, if that's your decision, this is my decision! See you later."

He turned round and walked off the field.

"What the hell do you think you're doing?" his captain shouted after him.

Joe didn't turn round, but simply waved his hand in the air. "I've had enough of this. You can't captain to save your life, so I'm dammed if I'm going to stand around fielding all afternoon. I've got far better ways to spend my weekends."

He stomped off to the changing room and slammed the door shut behind him. He picked up whatever equipment he could see and hurled it at the wall in a rage, before slumping on a bench and holding his head in his hands in exasperation.

"What's happening to me? It's a game of cricket, I love playing this game." He surveyed the damage in the changing room, it looked like a bomb had hit it. Gazing round the room, Joe began to realise that his problem wasn't just confined to his working life.

Jerry Pickford liked to make his employees feel at ease, when he had an important issue to discuss with a staff member, he often opted to invite them for a walk around the town with the individual in question. So, the following Monday morning, Joe found himself strolling around Sotherton with Jerry.

"I think you know what this is about Joe."

"I can have a good guess."

"Yes well, it's becoming a serious issue. I can't have a member of staff losing their cool in the workplace, and Friday wasn't an isolated incident."

"I know boss, I'm very sorry. I'm just having a tough time at present."

"At home? Everything OK with the wife?"

"Err, yeah fine I suppose."

"So it's work?"

Joe sighed, "I guess."

"Look, you are a quality writer and an asset to the Gazette, but you can't keep snapping at people and throwing your toys out of the pram. Plus, we've had a complaint from Vanessa Granger. Apparently, there were blood stains on the wall of her bathroom after your visit."

Joe's face turned a bright red. He tried to think of a plausible lie but nothing occurred to him. After a few seconds of silence Jerry decided to put him out of his misery.

"Look, I'm not interested in what happened. I just don't want it happening again."

"It won't."

"But it might." Jerry took something out his pocket. "I want you to give this women a call."

He passed Joe a laminated business card:

"Rachel Stone

Relationship Issues, Anger Management and Domestic Abuse.

Call now and get the help you need"

"I'm happy to let you see her in work time. As far as I'm concerned, if we can get you performing as I know you can, then I don't mind you having a few hours off."

Joe felt strangely relaxed about this news. Jerry was backing him and it felt good. In his heart, Joe knew he had a problem and wanted to get it sorted out. It was embarrassing to discuss, but Jerry had taken the lead and offered his full support. Joe felt compelled to do what he could to justify Jerry's faith in him.

"Thanks Boss. I won't let you down."

"What's your earliest recollection of your anger getting out of control?"

Rachel Stone didn't look like an anger management therapist. In fact, Joe thought she looked like a farmer. She was wearing tight blue jeans, a tartan patterned shirt and had hair in a tight bun.

Joe pondered the question, it was halfway through his third session and after a few moments of small talk, Rachel Stone had launched in with a big question.

"Not sure. I mean, I had tantrums when I was a little kid and a few teenage strops, but who doesn't. Brother kicks your football into the road, mum won't let you have chips, all the usual stuff. In our house my mum always listened to my brother and he was always right as he was older than me. After a while I gave up and stopped speaking up for myself even though a lot of things made me angry."

Joe turned his gaze away from Rachel and went quiet for a few moments.

"That was lonely," he continued sadly

Rachel smiled reassuringly.

The rest of the session was spent discussing various other aspects of Joe's life – his childhood, his relationships, his family, even his social life. She seemed very keen to find out more about his formative years and his quest to become a professional sportsman.

"I don't want to sound arrogant, but I was the best. School, club and district – I was better than everyone else. Right up until I was eighteen."

"What happened next?"

Joe took a deep breath. "I had a trial for my county, a chance to become a professional. I was going to make loads of money and play for England." He took a long pause. "Then they rejected me. Said I wasn't quite good enough and that they didn't need to see me again."

"How did that make you feel?"

"Angry." Joe's answer was instant and he immediately realised the irony of it.

"Tell me a bit more about this anger?"

Joe considered. "Partly I was angry at them for rejecting me, but mainly I was angry at myself. I'd focused so much on becoming a pro, I'd just assumed it was going to happen. My whole life was mapped out...so when it all fell apart I didn't know what to do. I'd been average at school and I wasn't really interested in learning. Who cares about Shakespeare when you're going to be playing in the Ashes in a few years' time?"

"Sounds like this really knocked your confidence."

"I didn't really know what I wanted anymore. I had a few agency jobs, dabbled in drugs and I probably wasn't much fun to be around. I felt as if I had lost my way completely. The worst thing is I didn't tell anyone at home as my brother would only have made fun of me and my mum would have taken his side anyway. I didn't have any close mates either but even if I did, you don't really talk about those sort of things."

Clearly they were on to something, so Rachel spent the rest of the session discussing this period of Joe's life.

By the end of the session, Joe thought that Rachel could be his biographer. Rachel explained that in the next sessions they would work at resolving the source of the anger issues and coping strategies and smiled reassuringly at Joe.

To Joe's astonishment he found himself looking forward to the following week's session. He wasn't entirely sure why, but he arrived for the session fifteen minutes early. He was interested in what Rachel was going to talk about.

"We all face challenges and difficulties. Getting positive outcomes from that is all about our approach to the challenges. You vent your anger, but in a negative way. You take out your frustrations on things around you and that leads to negative outcomes."

Joe nodded slowly. This was making sense, even if the words weren't exactly comforting.

"What we need to do is to get you expressing your anger and emotions in positive, safe ways."

"How do we do that?" Joe asked slowly.

Rachel smiled.

Over the next week, Joe came round to the idea that deep down his issues were stemming from that cold April afternoon twenty-two years ago. Had he ever really got over that rejection? Had he ever found another passion? Was he still bitter? The more Joe considered the questions the more he realised that his unfulfilled ambition with professional sport was the real cause of his anger issues. Which was progress at least, but he still had no idea how he was going to solve the problem. However, he had faith in Rachel. She was friendly, helpful and, more importantly, sounded like she knew what she was talking about.

"Lie back on the couch and close your eyes."

Joe did as he was told. Once he felt that he was in a relaxed position, he closed his eyes and Rachel continued.

"Now, picture an image that you find soothing."

For reasons he couldn't fathom, Joe immediately had the image of a butterfly in his head.

"Focus your attention on it steadily. Study the detail of the object, the colours, shapes, shades etc."

This lasted for around ten minutes. Rachel just slowly repeated her instructions until Joe eventually felt completely at ease. When the exercise finished, Rachel went back to discussing Joe's life, his past and his current issues. She went through some more relaxation techniques and explained how they could help Joe stop his anger from manifesting and hurting other people.

This pattern continued for a few more weeks. Rachel would spend the first part of the session passing on a relaxation or meditation exercise to Joe, then they would discuss Joe's situation and look for solutions. Over time, Joe learnt that it was okay to give himself permission to express anger, however it needed to happen through safe healthy methods. The running he had taken up in the last few weeks was helping as well as the relaxation techniques he was learning. Some of them he found a bit too leftfield, but some of them he found extremely useful. He was determined to use them when difficult situations arose.

"Hey Joe, got any more big exclusives for us? Maybe a local council member is into squash." Ray shouted the words across the office floor as Joe entered the room.

"Nice one Ray," He calmly replied and walked over to his desk. For the next few minutes all he could hear was Ray making snide remarks in his direction. Joe closed his eyes and pictured the butterfly, its beautiful colours, its graceful motions and its perfect shape. He opened his eyes.

Suddenly he couldn't hear Ray anymore, everything was peaceful. He typed away diligently for the next fifteen minutes, until his desk phone started ringing. It was Jerry. "Joe, can you come to my office for a few minutes please." He put the phone down before Joe had a chance to reply. He calmly locked his computer and trotted off to Jerry's office.

Jerry had his business face on and didn't offer a smile as Joe entered the room.

"Take a seat," he said solemnly. There was a thin, brown folder on his desk and he looked at it intently. "Now, you know we've discussed your anger issues and over the last month you've been seeing an anger management counsellor to help with that. Firstly, I need to thank you for your co-operation. I hope the counselling is going well. Secondly I had to report your issues to the publishing group as it was a disciplinary issue. Human Resources have come back to me and unfortunately we need to go through disciplinary proceedings."

"What does that mean?"

"It means two things. First of all it's an official warning. Anymore anger outbursts and your role here could become untenable. Secondly, it means that we need to have regular meetings to discuss your performance. That is until we have a track record of you performing well and without incident for a couple of months. Clear?"

Joe looked Jerry in the eye. "Perfectly clear boss. Whatever it takes, I won't let you down."

Jerry looked back at Joe. "Good, now get back to work."

Joe left the office and went back to his desk. He closed his eyes for a few seconds and thought of the butterfly again. He opened his eyes and thought to himself, "I can do this."

Commentary

Joe's anger problem actually started in his youth when he was rejected for the cricket team at 18. It is at this point that he needed to learn to express his anger in healthy ways. However this did not happen and there could be several reasons for this. Perhaps because there is often a stigma attached to showing disappointment, as this may be seen as weak and as a failure. Displaying anger is often seen as being a negative behaviour. It would have helped Joe if at 18, he had trusting relationships where he could open up and share his feelings. This could have been a school counsellor, a teacher, a parent, a sibling or a friend.

It is important to only share with someone you can trust fully and who will keep your information confidential. Talking helps to release it from your body. Also you cannot make sense of some things if you cannot see them. Talking helps to 'let it out' so we can 'see it' and make sense of it and gain other perspectives. Often solutions may not emerge from this but the process of letting it out and being heard is therapeutic in itself. Uncontrollable anger and depression are often results of a build-up of 'unspoken' emotions over a period of time.

Do you have at least three people to whom you can open up and bare your soul and who will keep this confidential? Someone who will just listen and not judge you. Think about this for a few moments. If you have less than three, then try this:

Make a list of everyone you know: family, friends, colleagues, neighbours, acquaintances etc.

Now pick out a few who are supportive and have listened without criticising you. What is the worst thing that will happen if you share your problems with these people? If there are no repercussions and this feels okay, then spend more time with these people and develop two-way open and trusting relationships. It is good to have at least three people like this as one or two may not be available for various reasons. If you cannot come up with three then consider using a professional like a counsellor. The important thing is that our feelings are expressed soon after difficult experiences, otherwise they build up over time and may get out of control like it did for Joe.

Also reflect on your beliefs about anger. What were the messages you were picking up about anger, as you were growing up from the significant people in your life? Were you given the permission to be angry without any consequences? Do you think it is bad or weak to be angry? Well, we are human so we will all feel angry in our lives at some point. We should give ourselves the permission to express it but in healthy ways such as talking to people we trust, writing it out (like Neil did in 'The New Man' and Paul in 'Built for Resilience') or diffusing it with relaxation and breathing techniques. Here's one breathing technique particularly good for anger:

Breathe out in short bursts with your mouth 10 times. Then breathe normally. Repeat until anger has subsided. Stop if you feel dizzy, let your breathing settle before you repeat it.

Jerry had the qualities of a firm and fair manager. He 'nipped the issue in the bud' and sought help for Joe before it escalated, as well as dealt with it formally. *If Jerry had not offered the support at that point to Joe, what might have been the consequences within the team? Take a few moments to reflect on that.*

THE NEW MAN

"The benefits of our course are peace of mind, feeling calm and relaxed, improved performance and decision making." Neil Arthur, Area Director of Breswell Group Engineering, was reading the content of a newsletter forwarded to him by his deputy, Richard. The newsletter was from some Stress Management company. Reading the newsletter made him recall a conversation with Richard from a few weeks ago:

"What's wrong boss? I've noticed that you have not been yourself for the past few months. Hope you don't mind me saying so, but is everything ok?"

"Oh, did not realise it was that obvious. There's just too much going on at work and at home at the minute. I am not sleeping, our new targets are playing on my mind, as well as problems with Mila at home. Can't really share this with our Mr Breswell."

"Ha, give it a try. What's the worst that can happen?" Richard asked.

"He'll say I am a wimp and to get on with it, which is what I am trying to do. To be honest Rich, I feel as if I'm at breaking point and not sure how long I can keep this up." Neil's eyes welled up as he replied.

"You need some help, I'll forward you this email that I got from a Stress Management firm. I looked at their website, it might be just what you need."

"Come on Rich, that sort of stuff is all airy fairy, and what do I say to our Mr B?" Neil exclaimed

"Neil, I'm worried about you, you said yourself that you're at breaking point. I am glad we can talk about this. I'll forward you the email, have a think about it."

Since that conversation two months ago, Neil had read the email several times, subscribed to further newsletters and sent off for their brochure. He read the content again. "The benefits are peace of mind, feeling calm and relaxed, improved performance and decision making."

"I haven't felt at peace for a long time," thought Neil.

He let out a long sigh and read the brochure again, then picked up his phone and dialled the number on it.

It was four weeks later and the office clock had just ticked round to 4:00pm. Neil grabbed his laptop and briefcase.

"It's been a long month I can't wait to get out of this office," he thought, feeling exhausted and weighed down. As he walked out, for a brief moment his eyes rested on the picture on his desk. It was of a young woman with finely chiselled cheek bones, large sultry eyes and full mouth curled up in a soft smile. How on earth had he managed to get with a woman as attractive and beautiful as Mila?

"Hey, Neil!" Richard was speeding up to catch up with him before he made it to the exit door. "Breswell has just called and let rip on the phone; He's not happy, we've not hit the performance targets for the third month running."

"Not now, Rich, not now. I'm already late getting away. This will have to wait until I'm back from my holiday next week."

"But Neil..." Richard's raised voice trailed behind Neil.

"No buts Rich, this time I am not cancelling my leave to please Mr B!"

Neil carried on toward the exit door. He did not see Sharon the receptionist's puzzled face, and ignored her question, "Are you okay Mr Arthur?" He frowned at the big sign that shouted at him from above the front door, 'BRESWELL GROUP'. He was looking forward to not having to look at that sign for a few days.

He headed swiftly to the car park, got in and set off. A wave of relief swept through him as the barrier to the car park lifted to let him out of the complex. A few fleeting minutes on the road and the memory of Richard's anxious face and the urgency in his voice took over.

"For God's sake, why is it so hard to put myself first? I need this break, I deserve this rest. Do I need to have a nervous breakdown before someone understands?" Neil ranted to himself and carried on driving. The busyness of the motorway added to his irritability. Everyone on the road seemed to be in a rush, from the lorry drivers in the slow lane to the executives talking into their hands free sets in their expensive company cars. The bleak grey of the tarmac stretched ahead of him relentlessly until another hour later, when Neil took the exit from the motorway sign-posted 'North Wales'.

As he drove along the flowing and winding roads, he did not notice the breath-taking beauty of the landscape with shades of orange and yellow which stretched ahead of him beyond the horizon. All he could think of was the consequences of not meeting his departmental targets and the massive overspend on his budget. Mila, his wife, crept up in his thoughts too and he was overwhelmed by a feeling of emptiness within him. Neil rolled down his window, the crisp fragrant breeze tingled his skin. The tension in his body had just begun its slow journey of oozing out, when he arrived at his destination. As he turned into the drive, he noticed the mountains in the horizon. On the left was a big, blue, two storey building with large windows. He followed the sign to the reception and car park.

"Welcome," said the young lady on reception. She seemed to be extremely happy, which perturbed Neil slightly, but she was efficient at her job. After the checking-in process, she added, "The stress management course starts at 9.30am in the Upper Suite, it's just down the corridor on the left. Have a pleasant evening."

This was Hill Valley Retreat and was nestled in the heart of the Welsh mountains. As he walked to his room, he looked out at the setting sun as it gently dropped behind the mountains. He paused, and took a deep breath, longing for the peace and stillness that had evaded him, not just lately, but for years. After a few seconds, he realised that a few deep breaths were not going to erase the build-up of years of stress in his body. At that moment, he made the decision to skip the introductory dinner and have an early night.

An hour later he lay in bed tossing and turning, peace and stillness were still eluding him.

"What am I doing here? Should I have seen Mr Breswell before I left? Will this course help me? Will I be able to face my issues? What has my life been about? Why am I always upsetting Mila? Why am I not happy in my career?"

The next day Neil sat in the last row behind the other twelve delegates on the course listening to Marc, the Course Facilitator. There was a wisdom and warmth to his words. He was talking about the concept of the 'Stress Pot' - the filling up of bottled up painful emotions in the body over a period of time.

"As children and even as adults when we are not able to process difficult experiences, these store up in the body and can cause health problems. It is

important to identify the related emotions and process these using safe techniques."

As he listened to Marc and joined in discussions with the others, he realised how he had thrown himself into work to distract from and avoid all his painful feelings to the detriment of his wellbeing. The feeling of exhaustion had crept up on him as his 'stress pot' had filled up over the years with anger and sadness.

"So, how do you spill the stuff out of the pot?" A delegate asked.

"The activity of engaging and talking about your feelings, releases them from the body. Also, writing them down freely, without stopping the ebb, is another way. It may sound hard to do at first, but it is harder and more harmful to hold them in the body in the long term. We will also practise relaxation and other gentler techniques tomorrow which help to do the same."

In the afternoon session of the second day, Marc explained how the traumas of earlier years can be replayed in adult life when the significant people in our lives have similar traits. He asked the delegates to pair up and discuss this. Neil listened to the lady sitting next to him - a marketing manager called Jenny - who shared that she had been fostered at the age of five and her fear that anyone she loves will be taken away from her. She talked of the anger and sadness of not having the love of her alcoholic mother. Other people shared their experiences of being bullied, labelled as stupid, losing loved ones and dealing with discrimination. Neil thought of his dad but was unable to open up to Jenny.

The evening sun moved in and out of the clouds, painting the sky in glorious shades of red. Neil sat by a small pond next to the retreat. He watched the light being reflected in the water, and as the insights from the day occupied his mind, his attention drifted away from the water. His thought train wandered uncontrollably into his past and life at home as a child.

"You've seen me work hard in my room for my maths and science exams, every night Dad, I don't know how I didn't pass." *He recalled the terror in his voice as an eleven year old.*

"No son of a headmaster fails exams, have you no regard for my reputation?" Mr Arthur senior, glared at his son and raised his hand, ready to strike.

As Neil recoiled in horror at this memory, it made him think of Mr Breswell, the company owner, who would glare at him in the same way. He was a very old fashioned manager, it was his way or no way. The company was a success, but it was hard to get along with him. In fact, for Neil, it was becoming impossible.

"No manager of mine fails to meet my targets, I have my company reputation to maintain."

Every time Mr Breswell's small, grey, beady eyes bored into him, Neil's stomach knotted up in terror.

"I am still trying to get my dad's approval!" Neil was struck with this realisation. "I must stop doing that and do what is right by me!" He hurried to his room, grabbed a writing pad and, as Marc had suggested, began to write out his feelings of anger towards his father.

'Dad, I am so angry at you because…' The anger did somersaults in his stomach until it eventually subsided. He fought through it and continued to write. An hour later Neil lay on the couch, feeling a lot better having released the anger towards his Dad. "I must do this every time I'm angry with something and not store it in my stress pot," he thought.

On the morning of the third day, Neil sat on the front row eager to fill in more pieces of his life puzzle. He listened to Marc intently.

"A good indication of when we have emptied our stress pot of the negative feelings is when we are ready to forgive ourselves and others for those experiences. When someone holds onto negative emotions it does more harm to the self than to the other person. Therefore forgiveness is more about our healing and recovery."

Neil felt comfortable about opening up to the other delegates in their small discussion groups. As he talked and shared more, he felt a great weight lift from his mind. Neil also realised how his relationship with his Dad had shaped the way he related to others, wanting to keep control of them.

That evening, with more of his life puzzle pieces falling into place, Neil sat down to send two very important emails.

Part of his email to Mr Breswell read:

"I know I haven't been at my best lately, but I just wanted to let you know that my head's in the right place now and I want to do my best for the Group. Can we arrange a meeting when I return?"

He then wrote a second email to his wife which said:

"Mila

Please forgive me. I realise that I have not been fair to you, bullying you to be what I want you to be, like my dad and Mr Breswell wanted to make me. That is the only way I knew to relate to someone. You can only be what you are, not what someone wants you to be. We need to have a serious talk about us and our future. I want to be a better person."

On the fourth and last day, Marc led several relaxation practices. Neil fully allowed himself to be immersed in the tranquillity of the process. This time the peace and stillness stayed with him throughout the day.

"I have never felt so relaxed in all my life! How can I maintain this feeling after today?" Marc guided him to books, audio and visual products that the delegates could use themselves after the course, that were available from the retreat in-house shop.

"I am at peace with myself a little," thought Neil as he packed up and walked up to the car park. He caught his image in the mirror as he got into the car and looked at himself in surprise. "There is something new about me," he thought. He couldn't quite put his finger on what was different, but he couldn't stop looking at himself in the mirror. He seemed to have less lines on his forehead and the only explanation for that was a change in his facial expression. Gone was the permanent frown, instead he had more of a relaxed, at-ease expression on his face.

On his drive back home, he turned up the radio and sang out aloud, something he had not done for a long time. He used to sing to himself at his desk, until Mr Breswell told him not to. "Mr B needs to learn to relax and enjoy himself a bit," thought Neil. He mentally composed an email to Mr Breswell, pointing out how he could do this.

Neil thought of all the changes in his own life that he could make to ensure he did not have a nervous breakdown and have to go off on long-term sick leave. "I need to do my relaxation practice every day, not bottle up my frustrations but write them out, open up communication with Mila and Mr Breswell."

When he joined the motorway he carried on with the singing, oblivious of the funny looks other drivers were giving him.

The following week when Neil came into work, he breezed past Sharon and much to her surprise, offered a warm "good morning and how are you?" He carried on towards his office with strength in his stride, a glow in his face and a twinkle in his eyes. As he entered his office Mila's face smiled at him from the picture on his desk. He smiled back at her beautiful face, his heart filling up with love and tenderness.

Richard popped his head round his office door.

"Hey Rich, everything Okay? I will see you later at 11.00am for a chat."

"Okay Neil, good to have you back. How was your holiday?"

"Amazing, just amazing. I feel like a new man," chimed Neil. "Please can you set up a meeting with Mr Breswell, tomorrow if possible?"

"Ah...talking of which, he said he wanted to see you as soon as you were in," Richard replied.

Neil decided that he better go and see Mr Breswell straight away, so he immediately headed for his office.

"I got your email while you were away, what the hell is going on? You did not reply to my messages on your phone and I found these brochures on your desk last week, want to tell me what this is all about?"

So Neil explained in great depth, how he had spent a few days at Hill Valley Retreat, why he went, how he had found out so much about himself and how he now felt like a new man.

"A new man you say." Mr Breswell ran his finger down the spine of one of the brochures. "Well, get back to work and let's see what that really means."

'What it really meant' was that Neil was more focussed and better able to relate and communicate with his staff. He realised he was working smarter as he was able to make decisions swiftly and increase his output at the end of the day. He spent the next few days engrossed in his work. He kept thinking about and using the methods and techniques that Marc had given him. He also focussed on what he wanted and how to enhance the reputation of Breswell's.

Commentary

Neil's scenario is a good example of how excessive stress can seriously impact upon work performance. On an organisational level it is imperative that employers and managers manage stress in the workplace to stop situations such as Neil's from escalating. In the case of Neil, stress led to poor performance until he was proactive in seeking help. If it is not addressed, at its worst, stress in the workplace can lead to critical mistakes being made, sickness absence and ultimately a rise in grievances. It can also have a knock on effect on other members of staff and lead to a decrease in staff morale.

In the U.K. managers have a legal duty to address stress issues and the welfare of their employees under Health and Safety Legislation. Businesses that neglect this duty often do not realise the long-term cost of this on all levels - profits, reputation and moral implications. Mr Breswell was not paying attention and was unaware of the costs to his company if Neil had gone off on long-term sick absence:

Some of the consequences of this would have been:

Cost of lost productivity while Neil was off sick

Cost of replacing him with temporary staff

Loss of Neil's skills and expertise and commitment to his company

Potential complaints from customers

Extra workload and pressure on Richard and the rest of team.

Managers need to know how to spot signs of stress amongst employees. The best way of doing this is to have an open relationship with members of staff and encourage them to talk about any issues they may have. Good communication processes that generate a culture where there is no stigma attached to talking about stress is imperative. Having a Stress policy and format for stress risk assessments will also help to have a framework for ensuring that all cases of stress are dealt with appropriately.

Neil did not feel able to talk to Mr Breswell, because the culture that Mr Breswell had built did not make that possible.

As for Neil on an individual level, it took him a long time to realise that he needed to seek help in order to alleviate his stress. Acknowledging that you are experiencing high stress levels is the first important step towards dealing with the problem. If ignored, excessive stress will affect your physical health, behaviour, ability to make decisions, your relationships and how you perform at work.

Can you identify with any of the below indicators of excessive stress?

Physical Signs

High blood Pressure

Nervous speech

Panic Attacks

Tiredness/lethargy

Upset stomach

Tension headaches

Hand Tremors

Rapid weight gain/loss

Constantly feeling Cold

Chest palpitations

Work Performance

Any change in performance

Uncharacteristic errors

Loss of control over work

Loss of motivation

Indecision

Cutting corners

Absenteeism/Presenteeism

Not taking holidays

Bullying

Criticizing others

Emotional Signs and Thoughts

Anger outbursts

Short temper

Crying/weeping

Depression/Anxiety

Panic attacks

Fear of criticism

Feeling out of control

Loss of confidence

Cluttered thinking

Memory lapses

Slow decision making

Difficulty in concentrating

Behavioural Signs

Out of character behaviour

Difficulty in relaxing

Increased alcohol/smoking

Recreational drug use

Neglect appearance/hygiene

Bored

Unnecessary risk taking

Frustrated

Unmotivated/Apathetic

If you find that some of them apply to you then you are displaying signs of excessive stress. If ignored this may lead to long term adverse effects on relationships, your physical health and your long term direction in life. Acknowledge this and seek help. Often taking simple steps and persevering with it will turn things around, as it did for Neil.

Neil found the 'stress pot' concept to be a great help. He learnt to 'empty' his stress pot by writing out his built up feelings and through relaxation techniques.

Here are some of the other methods that Neil used to de-stress on a regular basis that you may want to try.

Focus on your body relaxation

Slowly scan your body and relax all your muscles. Tell your face to relax, then your neck, shoulders, arms, chest, abdomen, back, hips, legs, feet and toes. Tell yourself to let go of the tension as you focus on each area of your body. Finally allow your whole body to relax. When you have finished, think of yourself as relaxed and calm. 'I am relaxed and calm for the rest of the day.'

Simple meditation

Sit comfortably in a quiet place, with your arms and legs uncrossed and breathe gently for a few minutes. Then choose a positive word that resonates for you (e.g. relax, calm, peace, love etc.). Traditionally, the mantra 'Om or Aum' is used in meditation so you may want to use that.

Silently repeat this word slowly. Your mind will wander off sometimes and that is normal. As soon as you notice that this has happened, gently bring your attention to the positive word that you have chosen to anchor your meditation and continue with this practice for 10-30 minutes. Open your eyes and stay seated for a few more minutes before engaging in activity.

Object meditation

Choose a beautiful object like a flower arrangement, tranquil picture or site, lighted candle etc. Focus your attention on it steadily. Study the detail of the object, the colours, shapes, shades etc. Do this for five to ten minutes, then close your eyes and visualise the object, its shape and features. This is especially good for improving your concentration.

THE MEDIATOR

Paula Hart had always remembered her first lesson at secondary school. It had been a Religious Education class and Paula could remember her eleven year old self sitting in the stuffy classroom nervously awaiting the arrival of the teacher, Mr Denton. The quiet rumbling of chatter suddenly halted as the door of the room opened and a bearded, middle-aged man strode in. He was wearing a terrible brown suit, he had unbrushed, greasy black hair and his beard revealed that he'd had cornflakes for breakfast. He walked to the front of the room, picked up a piece of chalk and wrote a sentence on the blackboard: "God loves you and has a great plan for your life." Paula was nonplussed; the recent death of her rabbit Floss had left her doubting the existence of a higher being. And she had no idea how the death of Floss was part of God's 'great plan'. Mr Denton turned round to the class and stared into the middle distance, he raised a finger and uttered one word, "But". As opening words go from teachers, it wasn't exactly inspirational, but the class were young and full of nerves, so they remained silent, attentive and slightly confused. He turned back to the board and wrote a second sentence underneath: "Everyone has an enemy." Paula then realised what was going on – Mr Denton was a very strange man!

Thirty years on and Paula Hart was beginning to change her views on the R.E. teacher's opening gambit. Over the previous few weeks she had started to realise that she did indeed have an enemy. That enemy's name was Mo Akhtar and he seemed hell-bent on making Paula miserable, angry and unemployed.

Paula had been the receptionist at Fairville Doctors' Surgery for fifteen years, and until recently she had thoroughly enjoyed her job. Her husband was a successful business man, so she had few financial worries even though her job didn't pay that well. She was helping sick people, making a difference and she genuinely loved talking to the public and making them feel at ease. She was a content, happy and cheerful lady...that was until Mo Akhtar appeared on the scene!

Mo had been appointed as the Office Manager for the surgery. The surgery had never previously had an office manager, but in recent times they had become increasingly busy, had taken on extra staff and reached a stage where the partners felt that the staff needed a full time manager to look after the administration of the Surgery. At the time,

Paula felt the move was pointless. Yes, they were busier, but that just meant everyone had to work slightly harder and chip in to help each other out.

When Mo came along everything started going downhill for Paula. He was a friendly and - in many ways - well-meaning young man, who had previously been an office manager for a private sector firm. The partners felt that his skills were transferrable and would help make the surgery a 'well-oiled machine'. Keen, confident and hardworking, Mo proved to be popular with the partners straightaway. However, his methods weren't to everyone's liking...

For a start, there were the daily meetings - or 'huddles' as Mo called them. The eight members of the admin team got together for fifteen minutes whilst Mo talked them through what was going on in the surgery and asked them questions about how things were going. It was all based around a big whiteboard that charted the performances of everyone in the meeting. "Performance?" Paula said when she first heard about the meetings. "The only performance information you need to know from me is that I'm performing at my best every day!" Despite the murmurings from Paula and other staff members, the meetings had become a staple of the daily routine. More annoying, were the seemingly endless streams of new forms that she had to fill out every day. Elaborate tick lists to demonstrate that she'd performed vital tasks such as locking her desk before leaving and not leaving any personal items on her desk. It was all stuff she had always done, but now it required filling in a form! And woe betide if she forgot to complete any of her daily tasks, she would be singled out during the following day's huddle and asked to explain herself. An experience Paula found to be extremely humiliating.

Even more humiliating was Mo's regular visits to the front desk. He'd sit and observe Paula dealing with patients for fifteen minutes, then spend a similar amount of time offering suggestions as to how she should improve her customer service technique. "I've been doing this for fifteen years and never had a single complaint," Paula would say. To which Mo would respond with a curt, "There's always room for improvement." This would often lead to Paula storming into Mo's office later in the day and the two of them engaging in a shouting match that had no real prospect of a result. Paula had taken the matter to the partners, but as Mo was producing good results, they did not take her concerns seriously.

Paula was a sensitive woman and these incidents greatly upset her. She was venting her frustrations outside of work, usually with her husband Matt. They had had numerous arguments over the last couple of months and Paula was worried that she was driving him away. She was also struggling to sleep, as the prospect of coming to work was filling her with dread.

"Penny for them."

Paula realised she'd been sat in the tea room at work daydreaming for about ten minutes. Lost in her own world of turmoil and stress. Her train of thought had been broken by her colleague Jill. Jill was also unhappy about the changes Mo had introduced, but she was a far more reserved person than Paula, and just got on with her work without actively complaining.

"They're not worth a penny," replied Paula. "I was just thinking about how crap it is working here now!"

Jill sighed. "I know what you mean, but I guess that's just how it is here now. We had it good before. Now we've got to be all modern and do all the modern corporate things."

"I wish I could accept that, but I can't. He talks to me like I'm a child; he's tearing this place apart. It used to be full of happy workers, now everyone wanders around looking miserable and grumbling to themselves. It must be terrible for patients. If it goes on much longer, I'm just going to walk out!"

"You don't really mean that."

"Watch me! I don't need this. We can get by on Matt's income until I find a new job."

At that moment, Mo Akhtar walked into the tea room. "Afternoon ladies," he said cheerily. "Hope you all had a great weekend."

"Yes thank you," said Paula, before making her excuses and leaving the room. She thought, "What's happening to me? "I can't stand being in the same room as the man, that's not like me at all."

That evening, Paula went out for a meal with her husband. He had decided to treat her in a bid to cheer her up, so they had gone to a beautiful fish restaurant in a small village near where they lived. However, Paula was very quiet during the meal and wasn't eating very much.

"Is everything OK honey?" Matt asked.

"Yeah, I'm fine."

"Well, you don't look fine to me. In fact, you look like you don't want to be here. Is it work? Or have I done something wrong?"

"No, it's nothing you've done. You've been great lately. I just don't know what to do at the minute. I hate my job and there's nothing I can do about it. It's all I know."

"And it's just down to this one bloke?"

"Yup. We're just complete opposites. I'm sure he's a lovely bloke when he's outside of work, but inside that surgery he's a complete prat. Not that it matters what I think, the partners love him. We seem to be in conflict every day."

Matt had heard the story on numerous occasions over the last few weeks, but this time a small bell went off in his head. The word conflict had triggered something in his brain, a recent conversation he'd had. He tried to dredge up the memory and recall who he had been speaking with. Suddenly he remembered; he'd spoken to a chap at a recent networking event. He had told Matt about his business; conflict management and mediation.

"It's got to be worth a go? I hate seeing you like this, but I'm sure this Mo chap isn't a total monster. You just need somebody to thrash it out together!" Matt had said the last part of the sentence in a jokey tone, but Paula wasn't amused.

"Do you think I'm over-reacting? That some stranger can just pitch up and hey presto we're best friends forever?" She sat back and took a large gulp of wine.

"I just don't see what harm it can do, getting in an expert to try and resolve the issues. It's often best to talk things through with somebody who's detached from the situation. Get some fresh eyes on it. He seemed to know what he was talking about…"

"Ok, Ok, I'll mention it to the partners, only so you'll shut the hell up about it."

Paula had assumed that the doctors would have no interest in paying for a mediator to come in to try and resolve the situation between Mo and the rest of the staff. She was completely thrown when both the partner and Mo had agreed that it was a great idea. But here she was, just three weeks later, sat in the surgery's small meeting room, face to face with a short, bulky, middle-aged man called Brian. Paula thought he looked like a frog, so she had to fight a temptation to sing the Frog Chorus, and she certainly wasn't convinced he was the answer to her problems.

He started off by explaining that he would be talking to both Paula and Mo individually first. He would assess their willingness to work together to resolve the issue. Then he would get them together, open up communication and explore options for a way forward for them. The ultimate aim was to get them working together productively and successfully for the betterment of the surgery. Paula was sceptical.

Twenty four hours later, Paula found herself walking back into the meeting room. Once again, she was greeted by Brian, sat behind a desk, looking like he'd had a hearty breakfast. Only this time there was an extra person in the meeting room. Mo Akhtar was sat opposite Brian. He turned his head and greeted Paula with a curt, "Morning", before turning back and looking straight ahead. Paula took the seat next to him and they both faced Brian.

"Right, you're both here because, as you're aware, there have been a few issues between the two of you and the partners here are keen for them to be resolved. Now, the good news is that having spoken to the pair of you, there is a good possibility that we can get you on the same page and working successfully together."

She'd heard similar phrases from the partners, but somehow or other it sounded more assuring coming from Brian. Maybe it was the fact that he wasn't part of the practice, or maybe it was just that Paula was in a better frame of mind following her chat with Brian.

"Now, one piece of common ground that was coming through strongly when I spoke to you was that you both want this place to be a success. Paula, you've been here for a long time, enjoy working here and have seen the surgery be a great success. Mo, you've got a fantastic background in management. You've identified some areas where improvements can be made, and tried to implement them. Agreed?"

Both Paula and Mo nodded and glanced at each other. Brian smiled and carried on.

"You're going to start by listening to what each other has to say about the situation. Mo, I want you to go first. I want you to talk about yourself for a bit and then talk about your job. What do you want to achieve, what do you want for the surgery and what do you think about Paula? Paula, just listen to what Mo has to say. We'll swap roles in a bit."

Mo started by talking about his upbringing and previous jobs. Whilst the information wasn't especially interesting, Paula was taken by how much sense Mo was making. When he spoke about the surgery, he sounded genuine and sincere. Paula found his speech compelling and heartfelt. He did want the surgery to succeed, but more surprisingly he spoke of his great desire to help the surgery staff and to get on with them all. Paula was beginning to see Mo in a different light.

The session continued with Brian skilfully using other techniques to facilitate the process. Paula could feel herself feeling less tense with the situation.

"Now, you may not need to become best friends or even good friends. This is about ensuring your patients get the best service possible and that you and the rest of the staff are happy at work. Agreed?"

More nods in agreement.

"Excellent." Brian clapped his hands together. "Let's get on with more of this! Next, grab a pen and paper and I want you to both spend ten minutes jotting down what you would like the other person to do differently."

By the end of the day, Paula was feeling a lot more comfortable in Mo's company. She was still convinced they were never going to be friends, but thanks to Brian's prompts and the neutral environment, she was at least seeing that he wasn't the 'enemy'. Indeed, she had to concede that he had some good ideas and knew what he was talking about. She was also pleasantly surprised that Mo had listened closely to her input and even appeared to agree with some of her views. She still found his dress sense, mannerisms and business language annoying, but she was becoming less bothered by these issues. She hadn't suddenly decided that Mo was a great bloke and her new friend, but she did believe they could work together at the surgery. And that was progress!

Matt wearily opened his front door. He had been away with work for a week and was feeling extremely tired. He had just spent five hours driving and needed some food and drink. Despite this he was slightly apprehensive about seeing Paula. They had spoken briefly during the week, but he was fully expecting his wife to be in the same poor mood that had plagued her in recent times. Therefore, he was somewhat bemused when he was greeted by a massive hug and handed a glass of red wine.

"I have missed you so much!" Paula said, finally releasing him from the hug.

"Good week?" Matt asked.

"Not bad. Now, you sit down and I'll finish doing dinner. How would you like your steak done?"

The following day at work, all of the staff received a memo from the partners. They wanted volunteers to form a working party to look at ways of improving the waiting time for patients. Paula immediately replied in the affirmative. She was determined to get involved in this project and help the surgery. Following her acceptance, she received an invite to a meeting later that day.

"Great," thought Paula. "A chance to show the partners that I can still be an asset here and I'm over my dispute with Mo."

A few hours later, she found herself walking into the very same meeting room that she had been in a few days earlier. She smiled to herself and reflected on how different she felt compared to her first encounter with Brian. There were a couple of other members of staff in the room, as well as one of the partners.

"Grab a seat Paula," said the Doctor. "We're just waiting for one more."

Paula sat down, thought for a second and then smiled to herself. Whilst what was about to happen seemed inevitable, she was also looking forward to it.

Commentary

Here's a reflection on some of the positive outcomes for the Surgery as a result of the mediation process.

Valuing Difference - *Imagine what relationships would be like if we all were the same. Quite boring you will agree. As humans we are all different and it is about valuing this difference. Visualise a plate*

of food where all of it is the same colour and taste. Yuk!
Now imagine a plate of food with different colours, tastes and textures. Hmmm...Tasty. Human differences add spice to life too.
The mediation process with Mo and Paula helped both of them to value each other's differences.

Speed - Mediation can resolve conflict swiftly, even the most complex case (i.e. group mediation) can be resolved within 1-2 days avoiding the lengthy timescales involved in litigation or formal processes which may happen if the conflict is not resolved.

Cost - Just think of the time managers spend in dealing with a conflict that has entered a formal process. Imagine the costs to the Surgery in the long run if mediation had not taken place. Paula would have probably resigned with a loss of an experienced, valuable and committed employee. It would have cost more in recruiting and training another person if she had.

Positive working relationships - Can you imagine the staff morale within the surgery if the conflict had been allowed to continue? Mediation fostered ongoing working relationships allowing Mo and Paula to continue working with each other. A formal/legal process would have rendered this unlikely and in many cases impossible. A successful mediation meant there was no loser (win/win) and this helped to foster positive working relationships within the whole team.

Mediation is a common way of resolving workplace conflicts. Amongst the most prevalent circumstances that require mediation are:

- **Conflict between peers**
- **Conflict between manager/member of staff**
- **Conflict between senior managers**
- **Group or team mediations**
- **Bullying, harassment and/or discrimination**
- **Conflict between an employee and a third party (e.g. contracted services)**
- **Change resistance (working patterns, work content)**
- **Staff appraisal disputes.**

Whilst situations such as those above sometimes need third party interventions, there are plenty of steps that managers can take to help prevent a mediator being required in the first place. Here are the factors that should be addressed to ensure that managers have the skills required to mend working relationships and improve the working environment.

1. Communication: No dispute can be resolved without people talking to each other. The more information that managers and employees share with each other, the easier it is to find a solution that works for everyone. This can be helped by managers encouraging employees to open up and be honest.
2. Leading the Way: If managers set an example by being calm and sensible, then others will follow suit. Problems often develop because people become angry, frustrated and upset. When people feel negative they are less likely to listen or see any hope of things getting better.
3. Individual Motivations: Everyone has their own needs, interests and motivations. When a dispute occurs, these traits come to the fore and individuals become entrenched in their way of thinking. Understanding these individual motivations will help managers maximize the varying talent within their team.

4. Healthy Culture: Managers can develop a preventative culture, rather than a reactive one. Talking openly about workplace conflicts helps employees understand that it's an inevitable element of working life and can help minimize the impact of these conflicts.

===

> If these interventions help you, pass them on to at least two people in your life and ask them to share it with two more people. I believe that you do not need to be rich, famous or have a degree to make a positive difference and contribute to the greater good. All that is needed is compassion, care and a little guidance.
>
> *Who are the two people you are going to pass this book onto?*

Acknowledgements

I would like to thank my husband Manu, and children Trishul and Poonam. All my family and friends for their unconditional love and support in encouraging me to follow my 'truth' and to grow and help others to grow with every step.

Thanks also to all my associates (we too are like one big happy family) and especially to Marc Kirby for his contribution to 'The Mediator' story.

Heartfelt thanks to my dear friend Jackie Jones for her support, time and valuable feedback.

Finally, an extra special thanks to Simon Day, my Business Manager - this book would not have been possible without his hard work and perseverance.